DEDICATION

To my incredible husband and our three lovely daughters, thank you for always being my inspiration and cheering me on as I pursue my dreams. My love for all of you knows no bounds!

THIS JOURNAL BELONGS TO:

I STARTED THIS JOURNAL:

___ / ___ / ___

I COMPLETED THIS JOURNAL

___ / ___ / ___

INTRODUCTION

Hey there, fellow journal enthusiast! Welcome to the cozy corner of The Real You, where we're all about embracing life's twists and turns through the power of journaling. Whether you're a seasoned pro like me or just dipping your toes into the wonderful world of journaling, I'm thrilled to have you here!

A Personal Note from Me

Journaling has been my trusted companion since childhood. From pouring out my heart in my diary to navigating life's challenges, it's been my go-to tool for self-expression and reflection.

In April of 2022, life threw me a curveball. Battling Legionnaires Pneumonia, I found myself in a fight for survival. The uncertainty and vulnerability of those weeks were overwhelming, but amidst the darkness, I found clarity. Surrounded by love, especially from my husband and family, I realized that my purpose extended beyond the confines of a traditional classroom. Teaching, in its truest sense, became more than just a profession —it became a guiding light, a way to uplift and inspire others beyond the school walls.

Facing my own mortality revealed a strength I didn't know I had, reshaping my perspective on life's challenges and reaffirming my dedication to making a positive impact in the lives of others.

Why "ME Time" Matters

Life can be hectic, right? We're constantly juggling a million things at once, leaving little time for ourselves. But here's the thing: carving out some "ME time" is absolutely essential. It's in those quiet moments of solitude that we discover our innermost thoughts, desires, and dreams. And that's where this journal comes in!

Make the Most of "ME Time"

Inside these pages, you'll find a treasure trove of goodies designed to make your "ME time" extra special. From thought-provoking journaling prompts to whimsical coloring pages, there's something here for everyone. Think of it as your personal playground for self-discovery and relaxation. So go ahead, grab your favorite pen, and let's dive in together!

HOW TO USE THIS JOURNAL

Go at Your Own Pace: There's no rush here. Take your time with each prompt and exercise. Reflect deeply, savoring each moment of introspection. This journal is your safe space to explore and express yourself without judgment or pressure.

Embrace Your Personal Timeline: Your life is a tapestry woven with countless threads of experiences, both big and small. As you use this journal, remember that every moment, every memory is a valuable part of your journey. Embrace your unique timeline, celebrating the highs, acknowledging the lows, and finding meaning in every chapter.

Make the Most of It: This journal is yours, and its potential is limitless. Use it in a way that feels most authentic to you. Write, draw, collage, or mix and match—there are no rules here, only possibilities. Let your creativity flow as you engage with the prompts and make this journal truly your own.

Reflect, Grow, Repeat: Your journey doesn't end with the last page of this journal. Use what you discover here to fuel your ongoing growth and self-awareness. Return to these pages whenever you need a reminder of how far you've come or guidance on where to go next.

Remember, this journal is a reflection of you, your experiences, and your aspirations. Dive in, embrace the process, and let the journey unfold.

Happy reflecting!

IT'S WORTH EVERY MOMENT

Date: _____ Time: _____ : _____ AM/PM

Take a few moments to reflect on why you chose to use this journal and what you hope to achieve with it. Then, in the provided space below, write a letter to yourself about your current feelings and expectations for setting aside a few minutes each day just for yourself.

When you finish this journal, there will be another letter for you to write to yourself. Compare the two letters to see if things have changed. It will be exciting to observe any transformations.

_____
_____
_____
_____
_____
_____
_____
_____
_____
_____
_____
_____

ABOUT ME

Date: _____ Time: _____ : _____ AM/PM

Let's have some fun! Use words to create a snapshot of yourself and your current life. It's neat to think that someone reading this later on will have a vivid picture of who and where you were in life when you wrote this.

My full name: _____
People call me: _____
My birthday: _____
My age: _____
Where I live: _____
Who I live with: _____
Pets: _____
What do I do for a living: _____
What am I doing right now: _____
If I could be anywhere I would be: _____
My best friend: _____
What I love about myself: _____
Hidden talent: _____
Someone/Something. that inspires me: _____
My happy place:
New habit to start: _____
Bad habit to break: _____
I feel at peace when: _____
This is who makes me laugh the hardest: _____
Number of selfies in my phone: _____

Taking Care of Yourself is Productive

YOUR DAILY THOUGHT

Have you considered how writing one sentence daily about your day can be a meaningful practice for understanding your life when you look back?

This prompt is your chance to share something whenever you're ready. Capture one line about your day—whatever emotions or thoughts you want to express at that particular time.

I am going to focus on me today! Let's go get a pedicure.

Date:

Date:

Date:

Date:

MAKE GRATITUDE A HABIT

Choosing gratitude can truly brighten your life and it can have a remarkable impact on your day and overall outlook.

Think of it like the "Your Daily Thought" exercise where you jot down one thing you're thankful for each day.

When you actively choose gratitude, you shift your focus towards acknowledging the good things in your life. It helps you start your day on a positive note and navigate challenges with a more optimistic mindset.

I am grateful to be able to spend time with my family and my bestie.

Date:

Date:

Date:

Date:

MENTAL HEALTH CHECK IN

DATE _____

HOW ARE YOU FEELING TODAY?
_____
_____
_____
_____
_____

HOW ARE YOU FEELING TODAY?

HOW CAN YOU IMPROVE YOUR MENTAL HEALTH?
_____
_____
_____
_____
_____
_____

WHAT HAVE BEEN YOUR THREE DOMINANT EMOTIONS THIS WEEK?
○ _____
○ _____
○ _____

WHAT DO YOU FEEL GOOD ABOUT RIGHT NOW?
_____
_____
_____
_____
_____

THINGS THAT TRIGGERS NEGATIVE EMOTIONS
○ _____
○ _____
○ _____
○ _____

MY RANKING OF MY MENTAL HEALTH THIS WEEK
☆ ☆ ☆ ☆ ☆

SOUNDTRACK OF YOUR LIFE

Create a playlist not just of songs but also sounds that represent different periods or events in your life.

NOW, IT'S YOUR TURN
remember to take care of yourself

5:30   -12:18

SMART GOALS

"The tragedy in life doesn't lie in not reaching your goal. The tragedy lies in having no goal to reach." - Benjamin Mays

How about setting a new goal? You don't have to finish this entire page today. The key is to set smart, realistic goals. Once you achieve one goal, set another one! Keep the momentum going!

Goal 1:

Start Date

End Date

My Why

Action Steps
- ○
- ○
- ○
- ○

Notes

Goal 2:

Start Date

End Date

My Why

Action Steps
- ○
- ○
- ○
- ○

Notes

Goal 3:

Start Date

End Date

My Why

Action Steps
- ○
- ○
- ○
- ○

Notes

SMART GOALS

Goal 4:

Start Date

End Date

My Why

Action Steps
- ○
- ○
- ○
- ○

Notes

Goal 5:

Start Date

End Date

My Why

Action Steps
- ○
- ○
- ○
- ○

Notes

Goal 6:

Start Date

End Date

My Why

Action Steps
- ○
- ○
- ○
- ○

Notes

Goal 7:

Start Date

End Date

My Why

Action Steps
- ○
- ○
- ○
- ○

Notes

EMBARK ON A NEW CHAPTER

This space is perfect for all those fun things you've been itching to try out but wouldn't necessarily put on your "Smart Goals" page. What exciting activities are on your mind? The best part about this page is that you can track how long it takes to try out that new thing, thanks to the start and end dates. Ready to dive in and make those fun plans a reality? Let's get started!

DATE	NEW THING	COMPLETE

DATE	NEW THING	COMPLETE

LOVE MY BODY: CHECK IN

Date: _____

Let's give a shoutout to our hard-working bodies! Take a moment to ponder how we can show them some extra love. Before diving into these questions, take a couple of slow, deep breaths. Remember, this is all about you feeling liberated and empowered. So, let's get started!

Physically I feel: _____ today.

This part of my body hurts right now _____

One thing I can do to focus on my body today.
_____

Water intake today
(Circle or color in)

8 oz   8 oz   8 oz   8 oz   8 oz

My current stress level is at a (Circle)

0 1 2 3 4 5 6 7 8 9 10

What can I do to get rid of stress from my body today?
_____

How can I ensure I set myself up for a restful night's sleep?
_____

Using one word, how was my day overall?
_____

IF YOU CAN DREAM IT YOU CAN DO IT

EMOTIONS: CHECK IN

Our emotions act as gentle guides from within, offering insights into our inner world. Taking a moment to heed their wisdom helps us pinpoint areas where we can be more compassionate towards ourselves today.

Date: _____

My current feelings can be described as: _____

The challenges I've faced today include: _____

Today's high point so far has been: _____

Lately, something on my heart has been:
_____

To foster peace or create space today, I plan to:
_____

I'm discovering about myself that:
_____

Something I have discovered about myself is:
_____

The highlight of my day has been:
_____

You know, I think it's the small moments that truly make life special. It's like finding tiny treasures hidden in everyday moments. So, on the next page, why not jot down a few of those little things that bring a smile to your face? And here's a fun challenge: once you've written them down, see if you can weave them into your week somehow. It's amazing how these little joys can add sparkle to our days!

MENTAL HEALTH CHECK IN

DATE _____

HOW ARE YOU FEELING TODAY?
_____
_____
_____
_____
_____

HOW ARE YOU FEELING TODAY?

HOW CAN YOU IMPROVE YOUR MENTAL HEALTH?
_____
_____
_____
_____
_____
_____

WHAT HAVE BEEN YOUR THREE DOMINANT EMOTIONS THIS WEEK?
○ _____
○ _____
○ _____

WHAT DO YOU FEEL GOOD ABOUT RIGHT NOW?
_____
_____
_____
_____
_____

THINGS THAT TRIGGERS NEGATIVE EMOTIONS
○ _____
○ _____
○ _____
○ _____

MY RANKING OF MY MENTAL HEALTH THIS WEEK
☆ ☆ ☆ ☆ ☆

Unleashing Your Dreams

Close your eyes and imagine a world where fear of failure doesn't exist. What dreams would you pursue if you knew success was inevitable?

Take a moment to reflect and then choose a way to express your thoughts:

1. **List Your Dreams**: Jot down all the aspirations and goals that fill your heart with excitement. Don't worry about practicality; let your imagination roam free.

2. **Tell a Story**: Write a narrative about your life in a reality where every endeavor leads to fulfillment. Share the adventures, accomplishments, and moments of joy you envision.

3. **Sketch Your Vision**: Use drawings to bring your dreams to life. Create scenes of happiness, growth, and success as you see them in your mind.

5. **Express Through Art**: Write a song or poem that captures the essence of fearless pursuit and boundless potential. Let your emotions flow through your chosen art form.

6. **Craft a Collage**: Collect images and words that resonate with your dreams and arrange them into a collage that represents your vision for the future.

Remember, this is a safe space to explore your deepest desires and aspirations. Embrace the freedom to dream without constraints, and let your creativity guide you towards a brighter tomorrow. Your dreams matter, and they hold the power to shape your reality. Let them shine on these pages!

Travel Bucket List

PLACES TO VISIT

THINGS I WANT TO DO

DELIGHTFUL FOODS TO TASTE

SOUVENIRS AND KEEPSAKES

LOVE MY BODY: CHECK IN

Date: _____

Let's give a shoutout to our hard-working bodies! Take a moment to ponder how we can show them some extra love. Before diving into these questions, take a couple of slow, deep breaths. Remember, this is all about you feeling liberated and empowered. So, let's get started!

Physically I feel: _____ today.

This part of my body hurts right now _____

One thing I can do to focus on my body today.

_____

Water intake today
(Circle or color in)

8 oz   8 oz   8 oz   8 oz   8 oz

My current stress level is at a (Circle)

0 1 2 3 4 5 6 7 8 9 10

What can I do to get rid of stress from my body today?

_____

How can I ensure I set myself up for a restful night's sleep?

_____

Using one word, how was my day overall?

_____

CHALLENGE
Social Media Detox

- ◯ The No-Phone Challenge

- ◯ The Social Media Cleanse

- ◯ The Screen-Free Week

- ◯ Take a Break from Technology

- ◯ Disconnect for a Day

- ◯ Unplug for a Weekend

EMOTIONS: CHECK IN

Our emotions act as gentle guides from within, offering insights into our inner world. Taking a moment to heed their wisdom helps us pinpoint areas where we can be more compassionate towards ourselves today.

Date: _____

My current feelings can be described as: _____

The challenges I've faced today include: _____

Today's high point so far has been: _____

Lately, something on my heart has been:
_____

To foster peace or create space today, I plan to:
_____

I'm discovering about myself that:
_____

Something I have discovered about myself is:
_____

The highlight of my day has been:
_____

SOMEONE INSPIRING

Now, turn to the next page and write a heartfelt letter to that special person. You have the choice to keep it private as a personal reflection, or I encourage you to take on the challenge of sending it to them. Expressing gratitude and sharing your thoughts can deepen connections and bring immense joy to both you and the recipient. Trust your heart as you pen down your feelings, and let this act of gratitude and reflection enrich your journey.

Dear:

MENTAL HEALTH CHECK IN

DATE _____

HOW ARE YOU FEELING TODAY?
_____
_____
_____
_____
_____

HOW ARE YOU FEELING TODAY?

HOW CAN YOU IMPROVE YOUR MENTAL HEALTH?
_____
_____
_____
_____
_____

WHAT HAVE BEEN YOUR THREE DOMINANT EMOTIONS THIS WEEK?
○ _____
○ _____
○ _____

WHAT DO YOU FEEL GOOD ABOUT RIGHT NOW?
_____
_____
_____
_____
_____

THINGS THAT TRIGGERS NEGATIVE EMOTIONS
○ _____
○ _____
○ _____
○ _____

MY RANKING OF MY MENTAL HEALTH THIS WEEK
☆ ☆ ☆ ☆ ☆

MY BUCKET LIST

1. _____
2. _____
3. _____
4. _____
5. _____
6. _____
7. _____
8. _____
9. _____
10. _____
11. _____
12. _____
13. _____
14. _____
15. _____
16. _____
17. _____
18. _____
19. _____
20. _____
21. _____
22. _____
23. _____
24. _____
25. _____

LOVE MY BODY: CHECK IN

Date: _____

Let's give a shoutout to our hard-working bodies! Take a moment to ponder how we can show them some extra love. Before diving into these questions, take a couple of slow, deep breaths. Remember, this is all about you feeling liberated and empowered. So, let's get started!

Physically I feel: _____ today.

This part of my body hurts right now _____

One thing I can do to focus on my body today.
_____

Water intake today
(Circle or color in)

8 oz   8 oz   8 oz   8 oz   8 oz

My current stress level is at a (Circle)

0 1 2 3 4 5 6 7 8 9 10

What can I do to get rid of stress from my body today?
_____

How can I ensure I set myself up for a restful night's sleep?
_____

Using one word, how was my day overall?
_____

VISION BOARD

When we can picture what we want our lives to look like, we're more likely to bring it to life! Making a vision board is a fun way to stay focused on your goals and dreams. Here's how you can get started:

- Explore magazines or Pinterest for images, words, and phrases that match your vision for the next chapter of your life.

- Cut out the photos and words that represent these aspirations to you.

- Create a collage by pasting them onto poster board pages. Or, for a challenge, go big with a poster-sized board and display it where you'll see it often.

Remember, the key is to HAVE FUN with it! Enjoy the creative process and let your vision board inspire you along your journey!

EMOTIONS: CHECK IN

Our emotions act as gentle guides from within, offering insights into our inner world. Taking a moment to heed their wisdom helps us pinpoint areas where we can be more compassionate towards ourselves today.

Date: _____

My current feelings can be described as: _____

The challenges I've faced today include: _____

Today's high point so far has been: _____

Lately, something on my heart has been:
_____

To foster peace or create space today, I plan to:
_____

I'm discovering about myself that:
_____

Something I have discovered about myself is:
_____

The highlight of my day has been:

_____

Would You Rather...

Circle your preference for each item in the two columns below. If you had to choose, would you rather...

Travel to the past	Travel to the future
Live in a bustling city	Live in a tranquil village
Have super strength	Have the ability to fly
Read minds	Teleport anywhere
Have endless money	Have endless time
Speak all languages fluently	Play all musical instruments
Have fame and fortune	Have true love
Live near the beach	Live in the mountains
Have a photgraphic memory	Be incredibly creative
Explore outer space	Explore the deep ocean
Be a famous actor/actress	Be a successful entrepreneur
Have perfect health	Have limitless knowledge
Live in a treehouse	Live in an underwater city
Be amaster chef	Be a renowned artist
Always be too hot	Always be too cold
Be a famous author	Be a respected scientist
Control Time	Control minds
Have the power of invisibility	Have the power of teleportation
Live without internet	Live without television
Have the ability to talk to animals	Have the ability rto speak any language

MENTAL HEALTH CHECK IN

DATE _____

HOW ARE YOU FEELING TODAY?
_____
_____
_____
_____
_____

HOW ARE YOU FEELING TODAY?

HOW CAN YOU IMPROVE YOUR MENTAL HEALTH?
_____
_____
_____
_____
_____

WHAT HAVE BEEN YOUR THREE DOMINANT EMOTIONS THIS WEEK?
○ _____
○ _____
○ _____

WHAT DO YOU FEEL GOOD ABOUT RIGHT NOW?
_____
_____
_____
_____
_____

THINGS THAT TRIGGERS NEGATIVE EMOTIONS
○ _____
○ _____
○ _____
○ _____

MY RANKING OF MY MENTAL HEALTH THIS WEEK
☆ ☆ ☆ ☆ ☆

LOVE MY BODY: CHECK IN

Date: _____

Let's give a shoutout to our hard-working bodies! Take a moment to ponder how we can show them some extra love. Before diving into these questions, take a couple of slow, deep breaths. Remember, this is all about you feeling liberated and empowered. So, let's get started!

Physically I feel: _____ today.

This part of my body hurts right now _____

One thing I can do to focus on my body today.
_____

Water intake today
(Circle or color in)

8 oz   8 oz   8 oz   8 oz   8 oz

My current stress level is at a (Circle)

0 1 2 3 4 5 6 7 8 9 10

What can I do to get rid of stress from my body today?
_____

How can I ensure I set myself up for a restful night's sleep?
_____

Using one word, how was my day overall?
_____

Favorite Recipe

NAME OF RECIPE

INGREDIENTS

SERVE

☐ 2 ☐ 4 ☐ 6 ☐ 8

DIFFICULTY

☐ ☐ ☐ ☐ ☐

Vegetarian ☐
Dairy Free ☐
Low Carb ☐
Sugar Free ☐
Low Salt ☐

INSTRUCTIONS

TIME TO PREPARE

REVIEW

☆ ☆ ☆ ☆ ☆

CREATE A MEMORY JAR

Welcome to your Memory Jar! This jar is a special place for you to capture and celebrate all the positive moments in your life throughout the year. Here's how it works:

1. **Write a Note:** Whenever something positive happens in your life, take a moment to write it down on a small piece of paper. Include the date, a brief message about the positive event, and then sign it with your name.

2. **Place it in the Jar:** Fold your note and place it gently into the Memory Jar. As the year progresses, your jar will fill up with these wonderful memories.

3. **Open on New Year's Day:** On New Year's Day, open your Memory Jar and read all the notes you've collected throughout the year. Reflect on the joyous moments, accomplishments, and blessings you experienced.

4. **Family Tradition:** My family and I love doing this too! It has become a cherished tradition for us to read our notes after dinner on New Year's Day. The best part is that we don't know what each other has written until that special day, adding an element of surprise and excitement.

This Memory Jar is a beautiful way to appreciate and celebrate the positive moments in your life. Enjoy filling it with joyous memories, and may each note bring a smile to your face on New Year's Day!

Uncover My Identity: The Essence of Me

Take a moment to reflect and fill in the blanks below. These prompts are designed to help you explore and understand different aspects of yourself

1. One thing that always brings a smile to my face is _____
2. When I need to relax, I often _____
3. A skill or talent I am proud of is _____
4. My favorite thing about myself is _____
5. One food I can't live without is _____
6. One thing that always boosts my mood is _____
7. My dream vacation destination is _____
8. The theme song of my life would be _____
9. One food I could never give up is _____
10. One thing that always boosts my mood is _____
11. The one item I always carry with me is _____
12. If I could learn anything in the world, it would be _____
13. The phrase I'm currently loving is _____
14. It warms my heart when _____
15. My nightly routine feels incomplete unless _____

WRITE A LETTER TO YOUR YOUNGER SELF

Writing a letter to your younger self is a powerful way to reflect on your journey, celebrate achievements, and offer guidance and encouragement to your past self. Enjoy the process of self-discovery and reflection!

Reflect on Your Journey: Think about significant milestones, challenges, and successes you've experienced in life.

Write with Compassion: Be kind and compassionate towards your younger self. Acknowledge struggles but also celebrate achievements.

Offer Advice and Encouragement: Share wisdom and insights gained from your experiences. Encourage resilience, self-belief, and perseverance.

Include Life Lessons: Mention lessons learned from mistakes or challenges. Highlight growth and personal development.

Express Gratitude: Show gratitude for positive experiences, supportive relationships, and lessons learned along the way.

Visualize Future Dreams: Encourage continued pursuit of dreams and aspirations. Visualize a positive and fulfilling future self.

Dear _____ Year Old Me,   Date _____

_____

_____

_____

_____

_____

_____

_____

_____

_____

_____

_____

_____

_____

CHILDHOOD MEMORIES

I always enjoy reminiscing about my childhood—it's like revisiting a treasure trove of memories. Here are a few questions to help you dive into your own cherished moments. Have fun exploring your past!

Photo from your childhood

Where were you born, and do you know any interesting stories about the day you were born?

_____

_____

Where did you grow up (city, town, country), and what was special about your childhood neighborhood?

_____

Did you have any pets growing up? Describe them and share a fond memory?

_____

_____

What was your favorite family tradition or activity when you were young?

_____

What was your favorite subject in school? _____

What was your favorite activity? _____

What chores did you have? _____

What was your childhood nickname? _____

Who was your favorite teacher or mentor? _____

What was your favorite childhood snack? _____

What was your dream job or career aspiration as a child? Has it changed since then?

_____

What is one lesson or experience from your childhood that has stayed with you into adulthood?

_____

_____

EMOTIONS: CHECK IN

Our emotions act as gentle guides from within, offering insights into our inner world. Taking a moment to heed their wisdom helps us pinpoint areas where we can be more compassionate towards ourselves today.

Date: _____

My current feelings can be described as: _____

The challenges I've faced today include: _____

Today's high point so far has been: _____

Lately, something on my heart has been:
_____

To foster peace or create space today, I plan to:
_____

I'm discovering about myself that:
_____

Something I have discovered about myself is:
_____

The highlight of my day has been:
_____

Happiness Depends Upon Ourselves

~Aristotle

MENTAL HEALTH CHECK IN

DATE _____

HOW ARE YOU FEELING TODAY?
_____
_____
_____
_____
_____

HOW ARE YOU FEELING TODAY?

HOW CAN YOU IMPROVE YOUR MENTAL HEALTH?
_____
_____
_____
_____
_____

WHAT HAVE BEEN YOUR THREE DOMINANT EMOTIONS THIS WEEK?
○ _____
○ _____
○ _____

WHAT DO YOU FEEL GOOD ABOUT RIGHT NOW?
_____
_____
_____
_____
_____

THINGS THAT TRIGGERS NEGATIVE EMOTIONS
○ _____
○ _____
○ _____
○ _____

MY RANKING OF MY MENTAL HEALTH THIS WEEK
☆ ☆ ☆ ☆ ☆

POSITIVE AFFIRMATIONS

I am capable of overcoming any challenges that come my way.

I am grateful for the abundance in my life.

I am worthy of love and happiness.

I am surrounded by positive and supportive people.

Every day I am becoming a better version of myself.

I am at peace with who I am.

I deserve success and will achieve my goals.

I TRUST IN THE PROCESS OF LIFE AND EMBRACE CHANGE.

I am in control of my thoughts and emotions.

I RADIATE POSITIVITY AND ATTRACT GOOD THINGS INTO MY LIFE.

I believe in my abilities and express my true self with ease.

I am confident in my decisions and actions.

I attract positive energy and good vibes.

I love and accept myself unconditionally.

I AM OPEN TO NEW EXPERIENCES AND OPPORTUNITIES.

I am resilient, strong, and brave.

My life is filled with joy and abundance.

LOVE MY BODY: CHECK IN

Date: _____

Let's give a shoutout to our hard-working bodies! Take a moment to ponder how we can show them some extra love. Before diving into these questions, take a couple of slow, deep breaths. Remember, this is all about you feeling liberated and empowered. So, let's get started!

Physically I feel: _____ today.

This part of my body hurts right now _____

One thing I can do to focus on my body today.
_____

Water intake today
(Circle or color in)

8 oz   8 oz   8 oz   8 oz   8 oz

My current stress level is at a (Circle)

0 1 2 3 4 5 6 7 8 9 10

What can I do to get rid of stress from my body today?
_____

How can I ensure I set myself up for a restful night's sleep?
_____

Using one word, how was my day overall?
_____

NEVER HAVE I EVER

Traveled Abroad

I have / I have not

If yes, which countries have you visited?

Stayed Up All Night for Fun

I have / I have not

If yes, what kept you up, and how did you feel the next day?

Danced in the Rain

I have / I have not

If yes, where were you, and how did it feel?

Attended a Music Festival

I have / I have not

If yes, which festival did you attend.

Written a Love Letter

I have / I have not

If yes, who was it for, and did you send it?

Gone Camping in the Wilderness

I have / I have not

If yes, where did you camp.

Visited a Famous Landmark

I have / I have not

If yes, which landmark did you visit, and what was your impression?

Volunteered for a Cause

I have / I have not

If yes, what cause did you support, and what did you do?

PERFECTLY
Imperfect

EMOTIONS: CHECK IN

Our emotions act as gentle guides from within, offering insights into our inner world. Taking a moment to heed their wisdom helps us pinpoint areas where we can be more compassionate towards ourselves today.

Date: _____

My current feelings can be described as: _____

The challenges I've faced today include: _____

Today's high point so far has been: _____

Lately, something on my heart has been:
_____

To foster peace or create space today, I plan to:
_____

I'm discovering about myself that:
_____

Something I have discovered about myself is:
_____

The highlight of my day has been:
_____

MENTAL HEALTH CHECK IN

DATE _____

HOW ARE YOU FEELING TODAY?
_____
_____
_____
_____

HOW ARE YOU FEELING TODAY?

HOW CAN YOU IMPROVE YOUR MENTAL HEALTH?
_____
_____
_____
_____
_____

WHAT HAVE BEEN YOUR THREE DOMINANT EMOTIONS THIS WEEK?
- _____
- _____
- _____

WHAT DO YOU FEEL GOOD ABOUT RIGHT NOW?
_____
_____
_____
_____
_____

THINGS THAT TRIGGERS NEGATIVE EMOTIONS
- _____
- _____
- _____
- _____

MY RANKING OF MY MENTAL HEALTH THIS WEEK

☆ ☆ ☆ ☆ ☆

MY FIRSTS

The initial experiences always hold a special place in our memories. Provide as many details as possible about the list of firsts below, including the year, location, activity, or any memorable details you recall.

Your first day of school:
_____

Your first job:
_____

Your first pet:
_____

Your first best friend:
_____

Your first vacation:
_____

Your first concert:
_____

Your first car:
_____

Your first hobby or passion
_____

Your first love or crush:
_____

Your first big achievement:
_____

AD LIB

Ad Libs are a fun way to pass the time, whether you're with a friend or enjoying some alone time. Fill in the blanks below with the correct type of word—noun, adjective, verb, etc. Once you've filled in all the blanks, use your words to complete the story. Try not to peek at the story until you've written all your words; it's much more fun that way!

1. Adjective: _____
2. Verb: _____
3. Noun: _____
4. Person's name: _____
5. Type of food: _____
6. Adjective: _____
7. Verb: _____
8. Noun: _____
9. Place: _____
10. Adverb: _____
11. Verb: _____
12. Beverage: _____
13. Celebrity: _____
14. Activity: _____

My day starts with a [**1.**_____]sunrise, which makes me eager to [**2.** _____]. I head to the kitchen to prepare a delicious breakfast of [**5.** _____] while listening to [**13.** _____] on the radio.

After breakfast, I feel [**6.** _____] and ready to [**7.** _____]. I work on my [**8.** _____] and then take a break to visit [**9.** _____]. I walk [**10.** _____] and enjoy some [**12.** _____] while taking in the scenery.

In the afternoon, I like to [**11.** _____] and spend time doing [**14.** _____]. My friend [**4.** _____] often joins me, and we chat about our latest adventures.

As the day comes to a close, I reflect on the [**3.** _____] of the day and wind down with a relaxing evening.

LETTER TO YOUR FUTURE SELF

Writing a letter to your future self is a powerful way to pause and reflect on where you are right now. It's a moment to capture your current self—your dreams, achievements, challenges, and values—and consider the path you want to take moving forward. Use this letter to outline what truly matters to you in this chapter of your life.

Think about what you absolutely treasure and can't imagine living without. What makes you beam with pride? What's weighing on your mind? What do you never want to forget about your life right now? And most importantly, how do you envision your growth and evolution? Take this time to be honest and open with yourself. This letter is a gift to your future self, a reminder of who you are today and the incredible journey you're on.

Dear: _____ Year Old Me,

LOVE MY BODY: CHECK IN

Date: _____

Let's give a shoutout to our hard-working bodies! Take a moment to ponder how we can show them some extra love. Before diving into these questions, take a couple of slow, deep breaths. Remember, this is all about you feeling liberated and empowered. So, let's get started!

Physically I feel: _____ today.

This part of my body hurts right now _____

One thing I can do to focus on my body today.
_____

Water intake today
(Circle or color in)

8 oz   8 oz   8 oz   8 oz   8 oz

My current stress level is at a (Circle)

0 1 2 3 4 5 6 7 8 9 10

What can I do to get rid of stress from my body today?
_____

How can I ensure I set myself up for a restful night's sleep?
_____

Using one word, how was my day overall?
_____

TIME WELL SPENT; LAST LETTER TO YOURSELF

Remember that letter you wrote at the beginning of this journey, setting your intentions for this journal? It's time to reflect on those thoughts. Write a letter to yourself in the past tense, considering the same questions.

How has journaling and tuning out the noise enriched your life? What's happening now, and how do you truly feel about it? Reflect on the benefits of dedicating more time to your well-being.

Date: _____ Time: _____ : _____ AM/PM

About The Author

Andrea M. Holcomb is your go-to Life, Relationship, and Empowerment Coach, known for keeping it real with a mix of sass, boldness, and motivation. She's all about helping you break free from limits, embrace your fierce self, and live life on your terms.

As the creator and host of the **Limitless AF** podcast, Andrea shares empowering insights on resilience, clarity, and confidence, showing you that there's nothing you can't do. Wife, mom to three amazing daughters, and unapologetically herself, Andrea pours her heart into this journal to help you celebrate your story and step into your true power.